A Holiday Gift

Level 4+
Blue+

Helpful Hints for Reading at Home

The graphemes (written letters) and phonemes (units of sound) used throughout this series are aligned with Letters and Sounds. This offers a consistent approach to learning whether reading at home or in the classroom.

THIS BLUE+ BOOK BAND SERVES AS AN INTRODUCTION TO PHASE 5. EACH BOOK IN THIS BAND USES ALL PHONEMES LEARNED UP TO PHASE 4, WHILE INTRODUCING ONE PHASE 5 PHONEME. HERE IS A LIST OF PHONEMES FOR THIS PHASE, WITH THE NEW PHASE 5 PHONEME. AN EXAMPLE OF THE PRONUNCIATION CAN BE FOUND IN BRACKETS.

Phase 3			
j (jug)	v (van)	w (wet)	x (fox)
y (yellow)	z (zoo)	zz (buzz)	qu (quick)
ch (chip)	sh (shop)	th (thin/then)	ng (ring)
ai (rain)	ee (feet)	igh (night)	oa (boat)
oo (boot/look)	ar (farm)	or (for)	ur (hurt)
ow (cow)	oi (coin)	ear (dear)	air (fair)
ure (sure)	er (corner)		

New Phase 5 Phoneme	ay (clay, say, way)

HERE ARE SOME WORDS WHICH YOUR CHILD MAY FIND TRICKY.

Phase 4 Tricky Words			
said	were	have	there
like	little	so	one
do	when	some	out
come	what		

TOP TIPS FOR HELPING YOUR CHILD TO READ:

- Allow children time to break down unfamiliar words into units of sound and then encourage children to string these sounds together to create the word.

- Encourage your child to point out any focus phonics when they are used.

- Read through the book more than once to grow confidence.

- Ask simple questions about the text to assess understanding.

- Encourage children to use illustrations as prompts.

This book introduces the phoneme /ay/ and is a Blue+ Level 4+ book band.

A Holiday Gift

Written by
William Anthony

Illustrated by
Maia Batumashvili

Wow. That is a big, big gift. The gift is for Fay.

It seems that the tree is under the gift, not the gift under the tree!

What might it be? Fay starts to wish her mum was there to help her think.

Fay's mum is away for her job. She will not be back until May.

But Dad is there to help Fay think.
"Come on, Fay. What is it?" says Dad.

"A railway!" says Fay. "A railway with 100 trains that go this way and that way!"

"There can be big loops just for mayhem!" Fay says.

Fay needs to relax. Trains must stay on the track, Fay!

"It might be a big blob of clay!" says Fay.

"If it is, I will form a big monster! Bigger than 100 trees!"

"It will stomp and crush and..."
Dad stops Fay. Good job, Dad.

"Can you think of a gift with no mayhem at all?" says Dad.

A gift with no mayhem is boring. Fay will not stop.

"Sweets!" Fay yells. "The gift might be layers and layers of sweets!"

"There will be lots of sweets. We will fill up a pool!" she yells.

"That is better," sighs Dad. But Dad says this too soon.

"Then the pool will go BOOM!" yells Fay. Dad sighs.

Fay needs to ring her mum and then go to bed.

"You do not need to ring Mum just yet," says Dad.

"But it is the holiday," says Fay. "Mum will be waiting to see me."

"Yes, she will. But come and see," says Dad. Dad and Fay go down the stairs.

"Go on, go for the big gift," says Dad.

Fay grabs it. She rips off the big top.
The bits of the box come apart…

"MUM!" yells Fay. Mum is back for the holidays!

"The best bit is yet to come, Fay," says Mum.

"I am back to stay. There is no need to wait until May!" Mum's hugs are good.

A Holiday Gift

1) What is the biggest gift you have ever been given?

2) Which of these was NOT an idea that Fay had?
   a) Sweets
   b) Robot
   c) Railway

3) When was Fay's mum supposed to be back from her job?

4) How do you think Fay felt when she saw her mum was the gift?

5) What job do your parents or carers have? Where do they go to work?

©2022 **BookLife Publishing Ltd.**
King's Lynn, Norfolk PE30 4LS

ISBN 978-1-80155-048-2

All rights reserved. Printed in Poland.
A catalogue record for this book is available from the British Library.

A Holiday Gift
Written by William Anthony
Illustrated by Maia Batumashvili

An Introduction to BookLife Readers...

Our Readers have been specifically created in line with the London Institute of Education's approach to book banding and are phonetically decodable and ordered to support each phase of the Letters and Sounds document.

Each book has been created to provide the best possible reading and learning experience. Our aim is to share our love of books with children, providing both emerging readers and prolific page-turners with beautiful books that are guaranteed to provoke interest and learning, regardless of ability.

BOOK BAND GRADED using the Institute of Education's approach to levelling.

PHONETICALLY DECODABLE supporting each phase of Letters and Sounds.

EXERCISES AND QUESTIONS to offer reinforcement and to ascertain comprehension.

BEAUTIFULLY ILLUSTRATED to inspire and provoke engagement, providing a variety of styles for the reader to enjoy whilst reading through the series.

AUTHOR INSIGHT: WILLIAM ANTHONY

Despite his young age, William Anthony's involvement with children's education is quite extensive. He has written over 60 titles with BookLife Publishing so far, across a wide range of subjects. William graduated from Cardiff University with a 1st Class BA (Hons) in Journalism, Media and Culture, creating an app and a TV series, among other things, during his time there.

William Anthony has also produced work for the Prince's Trust, a charity created by HRH The Prince of Wales, that helps young people with their professional future. He has created animated videos for a children's education company that works closely with the charity.

This book introduces the phoneme /ay/ and is a Blue+ Level 4+ book band.